The Essential Guide to Flight

Celeste Augé

salmonpoetry

Published in 2009 by
Salmon Poetry
Cliffs of Moher, County Clare, Ireland
Website: www.salmonpoetry.com
Email: info@salmonpoetry.com

Copyright © Celeste Augé 2009

ISBN 978-1-907056-05-5

All rights reserved. No part of this publication may be reproduced or transmitted in any form or by any means, electronic or mechanical, including photography, recording, or any information storage or retrieval system, without permission in writing from the publisher. The book is sold subject to the condition that it shall not, by way of trade or otherwise, be lent, resold or otherwise circulated without the publisher's prior consent in any form of binding or cover other than that in which it is published and without a similar condition, including this condition, being imposed on the subsequent purchaser.

Cover artwork: A detail from *The Long Walk Home* by Philip Lindey
Cover design & typesetting: Siobhán Hutson

The publisher and author gratefully acknowledge the financial support of Galway County Council toward the publication of this book.

Acknowledgments

Some of these poems have appeared previously in the following publications: *The Sunday Tribune*, *Poetry Ireland Review*, *The Stinging Fly*, *Crannóg*, *The Ground Beneath Her Feet* anthology (Cinnamon Press, Wales), *City of Strangers* anthology (Galway City Arts Office) edited by Michael O'Loughlin, *NthPosition.com*, *Smoke and Skin* joint chapbook (Lapwing, Belfast)

I would like to acknowledge the support of the members of Ed's Group, Mary O'Malley, Michael Gorman and the staff & students of NUI Galway's MA in Writing 2006, Jessie (for taking the risk on yet another new-ish poet), the Tyrone Guthrie Centre, Galway County Council Arts Office, as well as all the writers who have helped, sat beside, or worked with me over the past few years.

I would also like to thank the organisers of various reading series around the country for their hospitality and support, and the audiences who not only show up, but listen, too. Applause for all of you.

Contents

I

The Borrower	11
Opposing Light	12
Fired Clay	13
Stealing a Clock from Auden	15
Stockpile	16
I Dream in Solid Pine	17
Storm	18
Joan's Shadow	20
Totems	21
My Mother Tries to Knit	22
Song of the Sidhe	23
Where No One Can See You	25

II

Molly (the Golden Mule)	29
Judith and the General	31
Blame It on Breakfast	32
Rainbow Trout	34
My Youngest Son Came Home Today	36
Shapeshifter	37
He Wonders Which Scars Decide	38
Daughter	39
The Gap that Opens Up	40
The Sleepwalkers	41
The City	42
Fishbowl	43

III

Connections	47
Why Don't I Teach Him English, They Ask	48
Let Me Tell You	49
Piebald	50
Footfall	51
Find Galway, circa 1985	53
Stealing Rain	54
The Essential Guide to Flight	55
Nothing on My Lips	56
Lost	57
Wave to Wave:	
The Homestead I	58
The Distance to Lough Derravaragh (and Back)	59
Plastic Bags and Cigarettes on the Straits of Moyle	60
Erris, with Wings	61
The Homestead II	62

IV

Touch Close	65
On Contact	66
Before the Air Caught Me	68
Telepathy in Ordinary Lives	69
Watching a Bird Rebuild Her Nest while Slopping Out the Tent One Morning in Carnac	71
The Visit	72
Accommodating Grief	75
On the Fault Line	76
Who Knew?	77
Coming Home	78
Email Me	79
Fireproof	80
Notes	81

I

The Borrower

Do they know I would swallow them whole?
I have lined the bottom of my belly
with syntax, sustained by
vowels and skim milk.
Still the books submit their truths.

I have invented worlds for myself
from the words found in four libraries—
gained a family, learnt myself,
lost myself, consumed my own words.

The neat rows of print let me in,
never question my credentials,
flip open at the slightest nudge.

I feed myself on their words,
my lips blue-black from the ink.
Up close you can see the letters
that slipped off the page
imprinted on my skin.

Opposing Light

At exactly ten past one on April Fool's Day
the moon hangs outside my windshield,
a half-disc in a rare blue sky, a pale
version of itself, drowned out by the sun
suspended on the other end
of the sky blue glass.

The elastic light of spring reveals
the persistent bud of a daffodil
that will flower after the other bulbs
have got fed up of this year's show,
and the slowing steps of a granduncle,
how you suddenly notice that his life left
is measured in years, not decades.

And how this life inside of me
will not wait till I am ready,
will suck me down into itself,
into its blank moon head, drown me
in potential before one more
due date has passed.

Fired Clay

for Yvonne Green

understand *verb*
    to grasp the meaning, cause, or significance,
    of a subject, a person, a language

Stating the three possibilities you see
from where you stand,
the way your grown daughter's hair
can shift colour in a different light,
and have someone listen,
try to see *eat* as you see it

huge oval dishes peaked with rice,
brown rice, green rice, rice oranged with carrot slivers

yet retain their own vision of the world—
even add to it,

so like a mosaic the crosshair stories
of chromium, cinnabar, burnt umber,
add into the folds of one woman's sleeve
and those who are lucky enough to have heard
many stories, how

there is a different history to the tarmac streets and traffic lights

will be able to step back from the wall,
back from the glazed colours, the tiles
glinting in the sun, and see the blurred
vision this world makes—

discover *verb*
    to learn of or become aware of
    something or someone for the first time

and if you look from one angle
there's a white and black cow stretching her neck
out to reach the new grass at the edge,
and if you step back
even further you can see
the abstract pattern of arrows
that seem to point to the centre

stepping back

until each picture and pattern become
something else, the further you
step back, the more stories
get added to the fired clay.

Stealing a Clock from Auden

You see the touch of their hands,
the way a middle-aged man holds
the hand of an old man
who walks with a stick.

You start to feel a bit loose—
as though chunks of you could fall off—

simply from a glimpse of two men
you have never seen before,
walking through the automatic doors.

You see the touch of those hands,
and it seems a fire sparks
at the point they meet, and that same heat
burns in you, as if there is no you,
as if you are the space they hold
between their imperfect grip.

In this flash you can picture yourself
cupped in that cradle of hands,
safe and growing.

And you think how matter can shift
in the split of a second,

how for moments you do not hold
the divides of the kitchen clock world,
the sure touch of blue J-cloths
and metronome smells.

Stockpile

*'Let your poetry fill up
the equinoctial pastry shop.'*
           Pablo Neruda

If you open the pantry door
too fast, watch out
for the muscovado sugar,
the fine-milled flour
and ground ginger, almonds,
cinnamon sticks.
The tower could fall
with the slightest draft.

Study these treats:
peach crumble, almond tarts,
sweet paste fruit
formed with subtle flesh
and words with give.

You need a mountain of sweet,
built up slowly, over time,
so when your husband decides
he can no longer take
the trace of crumbs and butter
on your upper lip,
you can take the machinery
of your shared life apart,
piece by rough piece,

and rebuild that house
with gingercake and marzipan,
ready to eat.

I Dream in Solid Pine

The bed divides us. We take sides,
mine piled book-high with
balms, night creams, a clock.
His with books, a light, a digital clock.

We meet lustily in the middle,
then sated, roll back where we
came from. No place for sound
words between the posts.

The bed is solid, framed in pine.
It passed the shake test
the day we bought it, tired
as always, in a hurry.

The third bed in our history—
also the longest drop to the floor.

Storm

I wake with the pulse of three dreams on my pillow, wonder which one is mine. I lose my place in this cup of tea, toast crumbs leaving trails on the duvet, as if I could decipher them. The two boys give me peace before the caffeine hits, and the sound of their morning dance filters through the door, past the stack of road maps and wraiths.

It's the first day I don't know where I'm going.

Neither the swelling music, nor my Skoda, nor the thunderous hail that makes the car in front seem to levitate—its wheels clouded in pieces of ice, the air visible around each metal box like breath in a night frost—not one of these brings me out of my January box, instead shunting me home, a strong pull like the draw on a good chimney.

I continue to lose myself, my skin thinning with wonder on the worn grey ribbon of tarmac, the bridge to how,

how the shadow cast over my early backyard by the man with the voice is still with me, how his single line lingers past decades, and how the other pictures that filter forward are felt, not seen: the panic of fire-heat, the air shimmer as it hit my bare arms, the way the empty rooms lost me in the five-strong house.

Wonder pushes through the home movies, the split screen of windshield and mind, electrifies the return drive through thunder; and it seems the clouds sheering from the dull white sky could drown a woman, lift a car, freeze the rain so the world is masked by a rush of ice stones, and all that is left is me and this ballet of cars, the two in front I can see, their ruby taillights poking holes in the sky as though the natural laws no longer apply.

Everything is charged: the distance between my bumper and the car a length ahead turns into sky and the road I feel under my wheels becomes sky and even my breath is charged with sky sky sky—everything is charged: the ions that form at the bottom of question marks, the clatter of dinner plates against the kitchen table, two blonde heads bent over the mystery of a small lettuce slug,

how we have recreated ourselves to here, all leading towards this moment,

sleep keeping nothing apart, leaving nothing to chance, each steady breath as determined as the next, each heart opening up with the steady rhythm of blood flow, that build-up of memory released with each unbidden pulse.

Joan's Shadow

She loved armour and mysteries
and had there been chocolate in 1429
I'm sure she would have loved that too.
She loved fire so much she walked straight in.
And still she is celebrated because
she could fight and claimed to be a virgin—

even after she drudged through the mud,
her floor would have been spotless.
Yet another Catholic pin-up—
inviting each woman to be STRONG,
to do What Needs To Be Done.
No complaints, and perfect hair.

I'm left with my bill-scraping job
and my little girl speeding past
and sex when I can squeeze it in
between traffic jams and
peanut butter sandwiches.
And the thing that really kills me

is I would love to go off to battle,
traipse across boundaries, send letters
to armies, inspire a thousand swords—
but I'd want sex, lots of it, and babies,
at least two, and where is the saint
who could do all that?

Totems

(after Emily Carr)

The sun enriches these women—
standing like poles in the shifting light—
carved sincerely from mother wood,
each slash of the chisel removing
what is not needed, the shavings
scattered over stone and fertile ground.

They move without seeming to. Trust
that nothing has come to each woman
without loss, that each chip holds a name:
Ernest Is Gone, Rebuild Your Home
One More Time, Do Not Pass Go,
Do Not Collect €200, Sister's Turn Today.

The women wait for rain, marking
the start of the season with an expectant dance.
Their babies have faces like wise old men.
Big wooden hands cradle each child,
hands so full of tenderness, they had
to be made twice their normal size

to contain their latent gifts.

My Mother Tries to Knit

This is the day my mother decides
to start on Sammy's scarf.
It takes three generations
to wind the yarn into a tight ball,
so I am joined to my mother and
my three-year-old son by
this skein of multi-coloured wool
(improbably bright).
We avoid words, taut conversation,
that misuse of language.
Allow hands and thread
to say what needs to be said.
I am here now. But not long.
Unwinding the knots we create.

Song of the Sidhe

We stood on the tips of our toes for you,
trying our best to stand still, together.
Play stopped. For you: quiet and the listening
that taught us the modulation of each voice
through anger or fear or delight;
we trapped these sounds in the space between
larynx and diaphragm—our song call
comes from the silence of those years.
We felt the quills in our elbows grow,
we skipped wave to wave, wanted to get
out of these heads, to dive into the wrong
end of the lake, the shape we would take
hovering in the air above us. Mother,
the wind blew you away just when we needed
your voice. We heard our own stammer
skim the breakers, a splash into the foam of escape.
We took what we could: a flock of white,
the warmth of sleep, the word *us*.
Our new voices formed over the steep
waves of the lake, flight promised to our
reluctant faces, as if we knew our lack of place,
the shapes our mouths could make.

§

We stand together, heels butt against the trees
on the shore—our breath freezes before you
can fade into the air. The soft winds of the silent
years don't prepare us for the longest trip,
holding on to the rail from the door to
the lake edge, bound to your whim of escape.
Listen you say, as you press our ears
to the railing. *Listen to what the birds sing*,
as if this song is the only one strong enough

to carry you over that wave, strand by strand.
We wonder which mother stands with us now,
and this question connects us more strongly
than blood could, the invisible thread
that shrinks as we stop on the lakeshore,
pulls us together. We abandon our own games
and plunge into your useless instructions:
sing, keep your sense and the words
you were born to. As though that will be enough.

§

After the flight will we own our songs,
will we shake off this sleep? Will we
escape the bodies our mother gave us?
We shore up our nests with essential daydreams:
the bare touch of skin, hot stew, someone else's
tales to nod off to. As we stammer
from song to song, we'll hear the sense
in every wave—the listening years
won't suck us into the deepest part
of the lake. We'll soar, we'll let the night
terrors settle under new feathers,
bob us up on an updraft, past the white
plastic bags caught on the trees.
We'll sing from the same songs (time signature
and Dorian scale long incubated), the ones
we took when mysteries replaced our games.
The years we didn't sing, didn't know
we would ever need to, will bind us together—
each tail-feather of each one of us will add
up beyond the early silence. Count us:
learning the moods of three different waters,
speeding through the four winds, surviving
hurricanes and rain. Will this make us?

Where No One Can See You

The last time
I got up on the roof
was to clean the gutters.
From up here, I can see
a nest in the Scots pine.
I don't know enough about birds
to work out what kind built it.
The fake slate tiles
are slippery after the rain—
a restless spell to go climbing
up on to the bin,
over the lean-to, to find
a toehold on the gutter,
recalling when I could
slide downwards on to snow.

The edge scares me now,
the different possibilities
for falling—one misstep,
a cascade of knees and elbows,
a silent film in black and white,
sped up. Or the shock of swallows
diving past my head
for the safety of their apex nest,
my instinct to squat down
pulling me past balance.
Or edging too close
to the last half-tile,
unable to resist looking down,
leaning out that breath too far,
to see if I left the kitchen window
open for the cat, until
the length of my spine

follows the crown of my head
follows my nose.

I shut my eyes red-tight,
shut out the height,
shout for ten minutes
get me the instructions for flying.

II

Molly (the Golden Mule)

When I came back, the world smelt
of damp earth and rich fusty sweat.
Suddenly I could stop traffic, press
my friction-hot hooves into the tarmac,
clop across in stubborn time.

My day turned to the sweet focus
of skin on my flank, the rub
of a tourist intent on seeing
the boggy side of the mountain.
Avoiding nettles, the cliff sides.

The colours drew them up there,
perched on my back, each step a wish,
that phantom of brown carved out
against slate blue, the weight of purple
as the heather flared in peat.

Hill of Doon, they would say to me,
over and over, laughing,
their voices booming down the length
of my ears. I would practice the silence
I had learnt between lives.

What I have now: two friends
in the meadow, grass, enough to share.
A strong back and my mother's long legs.
Forget that my father was an ass.
I hide my own traits and turns,

a dangerous liking for sugar highs,
that fermenting in my bloodstream.
Haunted by an odd chromosome,
my spine holds one body at a time,
on the outside. A quiet connection.

So why shouldn't I take care of myself,
refuse to work past what I can capably do?
Why should I pitch my fierce back
into the ditch when I can stand proud,
ready to shoulder enormous dreams.

Judith and the General

Relieved to escape the black cloak
of my father's house, I took to the khaki
uniform like it was my wedding dress,
my thighs solved with rough cotton.

He taught me to shoot the women first.
The great General Hol. He followed orders,
squeezed twelve-year-old boys through
the sights of his exquisite rifle.

We lay like husband and wife. As if we
had a whole life filled with this embrace.
His dark form curled around mine
in the night, stone blind, protective.

I reached up over his head, brought my knife
arm down and sliced through, those years spent
jointing meat in my grandmother's kitchen
held deep in my grip and skin.

Wrapped my prize in a pillowcase,
one our heads had shared, soared the miles
up the hill. Joined my village, triumphant,
changed. Free of the men in my life.

Blame It on Breakfast

Remember the days spent naked
in my little pink room, the space
between us squeezed of emptiness.
Giggling over which limb to kiss,
we thought darkness meant night
and the warm bed we slept in.

Remember the first flat we lived in—
flecked wallpaper, all the bulbs naked,
the flick of a switch flattening the night.
We cooked up magic chillies in the elbow space,
felt each brush of limbs as a kiss.
We put up prints to cover the emptiness.

Remember how we rolled through the emptiness
of our first Christmas, you trapped in
Mayo, the flat silent, just the cold kiss
of damp December winds through naked
city trees. I hated the quiet and the space
you left, blamed you for each sleepless night.

Remember that big fight, the night
I stormed out. You almost cried, said emptiness
was for beer glasses and outer space.
Didn't take much to suck me back in—
a phone call at work, ambushed by your naked
voice—one word and I gave you my kiss.

Remember the day we forgot how to kiss,
so that going to bed together each night
meant taking off clothes, not stripping naked.
How our little flat gaped with an emptiness
we had hidden before. We moved in
angles, avoiding the corners of tables, and space.

Remember the first itch for space?
Me, it was the third morning that your kiss
tasted of bile and egg, and in
that count I decided—not one more night
rolling over in the flat sheet emptiness
of our double bed, our loathing dark and naked.

I wanted you naked, to press out the space
we held, the emptiness behind each kiss.
The flare of heat the last night I asked you in.

Rainbow Trout

Today's catch is spread out on a tray,
hooks removed and the useless gills
lifted from the chain the fish hung on;
a cascade of early summer lake songs
rubbing against cold metal and habit.

The flat round eye of the trout, the way
it looks out, as if to say *your fault*,
makes her fumble so the fish slips from her
fingers into the sink. *Damn fish talk.*
Should be a quiet job, cleaning fish.

Scales stick to the surface of things,
scraped off with a knife, catching the light
on the back of her hand, towing her mind
to summer weekends at camp, catching
sunfish off the lake and throwing them

back in, the sun lighting long days up
fresh as though twelve years old was a show
she watched just last night, every gesture,
every joke and canned applause
her own rainbow vision of home.

Speckled fish watch her, back to belly,
one eye up so she has to ignore them.
She grasps another trout, firm hand shaped
to the gradual slippery curve
while she slides out the guts, imagines

pink flesh cooked through, transformed, opaque,
a delicate bone in every bite.
Its intimate taste, like hidden skin.
Makes her think of her husband,
the close things she would like to do.

John she would say to him *lift up your
elbow there so I can kiss your skin,
all the way up the scent of your waist,*
his flesh flaunting over the belt on
overworked trousers, and she pictures

hoisting the end of his favourite shirt,
running her tongue along the bumpy
pale skin, exposed to her like trust.
She wonders would he blink if she threw
the fish into the sink, walked into

the living room, flicked off the TV,
crouched down low beside him and started
to kiss the length of his side, his ribs,
breathing in his graphite smell, her hands
balanced on his thighs, the tips of her
fingers still wet from the rainbow trout.

My Youngest Son Came Home Today

First I saw of him were his feet,
wrinkled from the unlit months spent inside.
It felt as though I was getting to know him backwards—
as if he was an old man, balding and furrowed,
easily quelled with the right drink, if only
he could find it. Something strong and sweet.

Running backwards into middle age
and the assumed pressures of mortgage,
mouths, work, foot in and foot out
and then back into adolescence,
that glorious time of sun gods and the satellites
of friends and new words for luck
and back further into cruel playground games,
then first steps to the white rail,
back as far as the perfect cruelty of *I*.

His cloud grey eyes will be the only part of him
I will recognize and he will grow a new skin
(the daughter cells moving up the layers,
changing shape and composition)
every 28 days, shedding the motes
into any dim corner he moves to.

Shapeshifter

I have been one man's three wives—
of course I had to die.

The first time, I just gave
up after the third night of dry heaves.

When I came back, I brought
gifts, four small ones, before I took off.

For my last incarnation, I took an indoor role.
Bided my time, learnt to sew.

Gifted to mind the kids, his bed,
he loved me less and less,

even forgot which scent was mine.
Flight was faster this time—

I changed his children, his life,
called his sharp wind down myself.

He Wonders Which Scars Decide

Let me tell you a secret
and with those words she stepped in,
filled the space left from the sweet side of me
(sloughed off after the last battle).

We moved without seeming to. The earth shifted and
let me see where you come from was all she had to say.
The paths of ancient ice floes decided
which scars we would graze.

At first, she seemed to know just what I needed.
Yarrow blossoms in my soup. A warm place kept
just for me. *Let me take care of you* she said
and her breath flamed the air at my face.

Ripe, grown into herself, who could see
the stretch left to go? Stunted limbs softened
her touch, a smile eased her face back to a child's.
Let me laugh with you and the gap widened.

*Let me have what you have, care
for your cares, see your house every day*
and as if she knew the draw of that swell,
spread herself into my quiet.

Daughter

I kept my voice and my reason, handed down
from the mother who left me, and her mother before,
and further back to the source of this line.

Lifted my chin higher with each curse, years
I would have to move, find new ways to say home.
Witch of the air I called *did you get what you wanted?*

I didn't—I questioned her directions, but followed
the path flattened before me, dried leaves and thorns
swept to the side. *Be nice*, spelt out the windfalls

that edged the fresh-cut grass, words I swallowed
to bring me here, where ice falls with the rain
most days. Apples no longer feed my weird appetites—

I need brisk winds, and salt, air with bite,
food for the strength that curves my wings
around the three downy faces I brought with me,

where I live by the skin of my feet and my obstinate
feathers, born to push through the frozen tides
where the wind doesn't want us.

The Gap that Opens Up

What do you do when the laughter leaves you,
when the wind has been knocked from you
too many times and you're all dressed up
and your little girls are in their best dresses;
when the tide makes sense,
with its pull, its tangle of weeds
pushing up against the pier
and all you have to do
is step off?

The Sleepwalkers

'Chaque époque rêve la suivante'
    Jules Michelet (1798-1874)

Eased from our mother's clutch, against the will of the State,
we walked in our sleep down the stained black tarmac.
Rage unfurled in our bellies as the perspex wall bounced
against us, a charmed echo that called for elbows, more stones.
The plastic charges hit our varied skin, and the quiet ones fell.
When we awoke, they washed us off the streets with a hose.

The City

You watched it all from the top of the Square:
the leaning on shovels, shouts for more sand,
trees moved out to the other side of town.
Warmed by the touch of Dutch Gold, you found
shelter beneath clear glass, a home
in the last bus stop.
                        Stepped out of the show.
Kept your seat during a cleanse of rain,
tried to ignore the outsiders squeeze in
around you, the toe and elbow shuffle.
Water dripped down to form a fourth wall.

Back in your old patch you claim the granite
behind the toilets. Only you can see
the blood stains on each square, the faded map
for belonging.
              You find the steps left over
from the last session, try out this new
way of walking.
                When your arches fail you,
you will sit and watch the early men
battle the quick grime, the pigeons scavenge
on Chinese stone, the young overflow when
the toilets are full at 1am.

You'll watch them mingle with the long sides of ghosts,
bumping into directions and landmarks,
         always moving.

Fishbowl

I learnt to swim today.
Lived 82 years beside the lake,
82 years old and I never learnt
to swim before.
Never needed to.

Left the hospital, kicked my feet out behind.
Four days and four nights I watched
the water rise, tickle my corns,
my arthritis, my bad kidney.
Couldn't leave my streets.

I stayed when the kidney trays
started to float.
Submerged my head, got my hair wet,
so the water couldn't wet me first.
Swam back the way I started,
my home close and flesh again.

I learnt to swim today.
Counted the boats on my way out the bay.
Counted the friends I'd made.

III

Connections

Think of the word
genealogy.

Picture millennia of people
in grubby teeshirts and jeans
trooping back to the place
(they believe)
their blood-line originated
after wandering the world
through generations, shifting
plateaux, back and forth
for the biggest plate.

See this little lump
of would-be island,
still connected
to the continent, a steady
stream of early women and men
wandering back over the bridge,
back to the edge of the sea,
to find that little handful
of dirt their mother
called home, still looking.

Why Don't I Teach Him English, They Ask

Of course I want him to speak my language,
share with my blood the subtleties I know.

I want to use the rhythms of my childhood
in my own kitchen, in the rooms of my child;

for my boy to learn me through my words,
the same words my mother taught to me,

the understanding of me a gift she gave herself.
I crave the same understanding of my young son,

so every word he utters becomes a pact,
a promise between our split, the divide of his birth,

his need to draw breath. So the day his cry
transforms to Ma-ma, I will know

what he needs, will be able to prove it,
whatever piece of our world he calls for.

So our shared words will echo
the cadence of our unknown selves,

the music of the rooms I have lived in before.

Let Me Tell You

Every day of the year
for thirty-one grown years
I have been licked by these waves,
teased by the cold sand,
always damp.

The people in my dreams
no longer speak my language.
My bones ache, grey through,
and I long for the blind chill of snow,
the cushion of goose-down.

Let me tell you, you would need
to be made of stern stuff
to move to this island.

Piebald

I know how to talk like everyone else,
put on my work voice for eight whole hours,
smother the open fire, not let the horse
out of the back garden, keep the sounds
of the road close to my ear, like a shell.

Footfall

Our shadows stretch ahead of us.
The cool November yellow
reminds us of Florian's feast day,
the way we can laugh at anything.
I carry her handbag, wonder at how
such a small vessel can weigh
so much, how such a small shoulder
can carry this much around,
footfall after footfall, and I promise
to take her to the first coffee shop
I can find after we call to the church,
check the notices and add our own—
looking for work, good English,
hardworking, optimistic. She kisses
this handwritten sheet for luck then pins it
to the board, leaving behind a piece of her
spirit; and we walk to the next source,
refill ourselves with held hands
and petrol station coffee.

The steam swirls between cold
and the next day of work, and we step
over that low wall, leave the forecourt,
laugh at the sight of a fully robed monk
who carries a sign for the last
pizzeria before Oughterard,
and we can't even pronounce
that place, but we laugh anyway,
that early morning tickle laugh that lasts
all day when the woman you love
is holding your hand and you can't see
past the length of your shadow
on a low-sun day in Galway in November,
when you can't see the long grey days

that will pull down the winter,
the way the rain will get everywhere
and black streets turn grey, slick
with rain, thinking you're strong
and can walk all day.

Find Galway, circa 1985

Look up, the wind could be stronger, see the gargoyles on Lynch's Castle and St. Nick's, see how the railings around the church are the perfect height to lean against and see the goth-black boys, their long coats like wings in the wind of mid-December, follow them up to Brambles Café, past McCambridges (closed because it's lunchtime) and did you know McCambridges sells the only bottle of Heinz ketchup in town, or that the Square turns into Williamsgate Street turns into Shop Street turns into Mainguard Street or High Street depending on the way you go? Ask me where river ends and tide begins. Ask me the name of the city councillor who voted against nudity, the shop that takes butter vouchers for cigarettes. These are the subtleties I have earned: that *to pass the time of day* means to stop for the moment it takes to dissect the weather with someone you have met at least once. How a good hood works better than an umbrella in these medieval-sized streets, and the way the cars have to stop for you—it's a Galway law—and you cross the road whenever you need to, higgledy-piggledy, to get to O'Brien's for the news, to give a wide berth to Una's dogs and the cars that are trying to avoid these tails and do you know the exact point where Dennis harasses the tourists and Elvis sings for me, never falling off his bike, right there where Williamsgate Street turns into Shop Street; and you keep going, on past Holland's and Deacy's and McDonagh's, past the fresh fish and the vision of future pints outside the Quays on a rare warm night, keep going down past the Spanish Arch, the Basin, the Long Walk, out to the pull of salt and look I am thirteen, one year here, I am the water, I am the blackweed tangled up by the tides, I am pulled by the tides, a foreign body obeying the tug of the moon, I am the rough thin strip of sand left, I am the stink of rotting seaweed and sewage, I am faster than the walk out to Mutton Island, I am spring tides washing ashore the city's flotsam: Supermacs bags, illicit condoms, jobless blocklayers, dreamers.
I am Galway.

Stealing Rain

I'm tracking weather fronts again,
looking for low pressure cues
from Francis, my favourite weatherman.

The way a wind can veer across boundaries,
rip up the roof-tiles in two countries overnight
reminds me I haven't emailed God this week.

God (I'll say), this week I'll appropriate
speed-talking, an appreciation of floury spuds
and the knowledge of walking,

how to get there and how to forget.
I'll hang on to this stolen connection,
to the taste of Tayto crisps, salty rashers,

the lilt in the island's weather,
as though it had a mind to change, twirl me
like a blown leaf around my fallen home.

And God (I'll say), today I'll seize
the Gulf Stream, the early spring it brings,
the last of the memory storms.

The Essential Guide to Flight

I've been abandoning a continent slowly,
for twenty-two years now, standing in a room
without language. One step outside
and the weather wraps itself around me,
steals back a loose vowel, the phone number
of my childhood home, whatever it can get away with.

Nothing on My Lips

Wearing only my English language,
I lament the inflections my voice can't reach,
how my words don't skitter off or
surprise me, shame passed on from
mother to daughter to granddaughter
so by the time it passed my lips, I didn't know
what I was looking down on.

Mind your tongue, my mother used to say.
*Don't pretend the pond is the sea
or that our dog Jack can speak French.*
It wasn't smart to use strange conjunctions.
Remember the eleventh commandment:
find safety in numbers. But math lost me
somewhere in Miss Gibbons' class when

train A started to go in a different direction
to train B. I'm still looking for the platform,
watching the high-heeled women take
their places while I try on different characters,
to find one who fits—the head-held-up me,
glamorous words tumbling under my tongue,
with nothing on my lips but Cherry Stain.

Lost

Leave behind the desires of your feet:
the myth of home will carry you
through the maze of towering pines
on the edge of a paper town,
past Wawa, Blind River, Webbwood,
through bewildered years of motherhood,
three house moves within thirty miles
and the unfamiliar life of a wife.

Hear the promises carried on a song:
I'll take you home again Kathleen,
across the ocean wild and wide.
Play it on your Electrohome over and over,
twirl in pointy-toed kitten heels
to where your heart will feel no pain;
in-flight prayers pulling you home, where
you no longer speak the language.

Go quickly, gather up the precious scraps:
three girls, with enough life between them
to tiptoe the beach for live crabs and jellyfish.
Tuck the three things you have learnt
into the pouch on your back and fly
clear across the Atlantic Ocean—
geography stripping back with each mile,
creating a brood of wayless daughters.

Wave to Wave

1

The Homestead I
(White Field Hill)

It takes one breath
to disassemble a family.
It's that simple.
The parts that look hard—
packing dishes in newsprint,
putting wheels on the trailer
that will hold the important ones,
feeding the dog for the last time—
happen long after the real move
has already occurred,
that shift in breath that moves us apart,
scatters us across choppy water,
while each one of us becomes
someone else.

2

The Distance to Lough Derravaragh (and Back)

Memory brings each name,
the shape of each roof pitch,
the spiked outline of the winter sky.
They stay with us as long as we hear
each other's voices (like lifting
a long-ago shell to our ears)
and sing to them in the night-time
from the edge of the harbour
we moved into, so that the recollection
of this music is enough to satisfy
the whole race of men,
even the ones left behind.

Our imagination prays for that moment
of contact. We bring the strong
people with us, along with
their sadness. These fragments
are a bridge back to the world
we have left—the scent of freshly
cut birch, the contraction of a single
vowel sound—the world we were born
from, the world we could lose unless
every leaving is connected by this question:
'Have you packed your sense,
your voice and your language?'

3

Plastic Bags and Cigarettes on the Straits of Moyle

'Can you feel that wind breath?
The clouds look like dark smoke filling up the sky.'

We would stand on the ridge of the bay,
open our arms out wide and shout
until the air left our lungs, jump up
with each exuberant howl at the wind
as it droned off the salt waves, the same
way we would greet the move
into every new storm, howling
back at any gust that would try to blow us
from the seal-grey stone that marked
the place we could go to start over.

4

Erris, with Wings

What is this place, where we are fully apart
from the world of men, without a chance that we'll hear
the voices we know, fed up of our own,
where the sea always pushes us

up and then down, always the weight
of this colourless weather so every day
blurs into pure grey and 300 years
go by without any mind of time?

If you looked at us, curled into the side of a wave,
you would take out your camera, snap this moment
as if we knew beauty, as if we held choice.

5

The Homestead II

I know two granite houses: the tower my mother came from,
moved to the cusp of my father's tumbledown life.
When should I stop calling that home?

The sea clings to me now, droplets of salt water
dripping easily from my cheek, my hem.
Barnacles stick to my knuckles, the underside
of my feet, making work more difficult, stiff
movements replacing me. I used to be smooth.

When should I start calling this home?
Remains of the city, the people I lived with,
keep calling me.

IV

Touch Close

Breaking space—we begin and
the Arctic Ocean is between us.
We squeeze that space until
the prints of our bodies meld,
pressing out the seven
names for blue we will learn.

I hold your hand between
two dreams of what could be
and the words we will use and already
I am losing myself, forgetting
the world where you were not,
forgetting years where I
did not hold your hand
and that we began separately,
a plate-drift apart.

This is your nose close to mine,
your eyelashes grazing my cheek,
my careful breaths. I watch your eyes
move in sleep and I forget
to tell you the colours I see—
the red flags and yellow love
tainted to run orange.

And what we will do to each other
on the days without colour.
Okay I don't forget but
I don't want to shock this
pure hold, skin on skin,
where we begin.

On Contact

1

He untangles his leg
from the sheet as he sleeps.
In sleep, everything can be undone.
His wedding leaves an impression
on his ring finger; a reminder
of things he can't get away from.

For one night he chooses release
from the usual words, the phrases
that come out fully formed
over orange juice and tea.
He turns over and over, stretches
in this slack unpredictability.
Not his usual side of the bed,
no given name, no tags
to tack him down. Sleep load-free.
A chance to escape himself;
he's measured only in the places
where skin meets.

2

Her breath catches on contact, where
her diaphragm moves in her chest.
She knows no one will notice
the groove on her left index finger.
Comfort coming from the fact
that no one will care.

Her sleep is light, always ready
to speak to the needs of others.
She allows herself to submerge
into strong thighs and a thick neck.

To lose her name,
to not know where dinner will come from.
Forgets to listen for the words,
no longer a magic mirror.
Slackens off the taut reins
around her other selves.
She doesn't have to think before she
moves against his unfamiliar sleep.

3

They meet once, in the night,
both free to whisper dreams,
their pillows heavy with truth.

Before the Air Caught Me

It started slowly—melancholia
came over me first, seeping
into the molecules of my brain.

Three times I took to the bed—
carmine fever, then nephritis,
inflammation of the heart—

asleep from the weight
of alone and five mouths
in my upstairs mirror.

What I saw when I woke up:
a man with his children,
none of them mine.

This is the life I've been given to.
Birch smoke, the turning
of wheels, sulphuric air.

More than a gestation,
it was a year spent hiding
knives under thick blocks of wood,

in case sense told me
to use them. That same sense
could bring me

the candle beside our first bed,
the way we used to dance
and have the best fights.

I measure the breaths between
side-flips. This life could be mine.
Every one of them could.

Telepathy in Ordinary Lives

> *'Like atoms, like suns, like galaxies, our spirits are systems of forces which vibrate continually to each other's attractive power.'*
> Frederic William Henry Myers (1843-1901)

Sunlight builds up heat outside the flat-pack houses,
and the cries of small children cut the stillness.
The soft call of your own stare reflex

pulls you out through the grey newspaper,
reminds you of the twitching window audience—
a whole street long—and the time you were shattered

by the one word that cut past
what you wanted everyone to think.
Bastard.

And you were the first one to say it
out loud, quickly followed by *I could have
had anyone you ugly bastard.*

Oh that the tarmac could open up
underneath your toes, provide a soft landing,
give you a rest from the bone crush sadness

so the Porn Queen could kneel down to lick
the piece of road you fell into,
reminding you of the connection between worlds

until you would skate right back up, enticed
by her dizzy breath—
and the closer you'd move to those lips

the clearer the other faces would become,
features pulled through the page 1000 years
or 1000 miles from this inky day,

as if your dog would sense you coming home,
twitch his head to the knowledge
of your footstep, and you would take my hand

here on Lee Valley Road, we would open our eyes,
stop to listen, stock still in time, the way we do
when we know we're being watched.

Watching a Bird Rebuild Her Nest while Slopping Out the Tent One Morning in Carnac

It's like the time we squeezed into the Mini
for our first trip to Bundoran—two families
of five cousins, two aunts, an honorary uncle—
stuffed into a shiny red Mini with open windows
for the carsick trip to the coast.

We didn't mention the ghosts that forced us
to keep the windows down for extra air,
the breeze rushing past our daily secrets.
Flight gave us extra powers, magic spells
for the missing father, the lost thumb,
replacing prayers to Saint Anthony. The red shone
around us, our halo, and we were canons
and powder kegs, we would blow up the soldiers,
take their guns; we would show them
the fresh tarmac on the road to Bundoran,

how you could get in or out of a wee small door
into the living room of a family 3000 miles away.
How they couldn't pronounce your name.
How they would wait for the sound of bulldozers
and shelling before they would slip out through
their own red doors and together how together
we would end up going through the one small red door
shiny into the same world, the small one,
the same one for all of us, with the same sign
hung out of the broken televisions piled up high,
a mountain of glass tubes and plastic boxes,
burrows and birds nests made of plastic cable,
the same mountain and the same sign,
Welcome Home.

The Visit

1

I focus on her hair—
a strip-light sheen, three weeks
past the usual trim, except
that one patch at the back
of her neat skull—and try to
ignore the tubes and equipment
in close reach. Her prickly scalp
shows through the combed out bits
when she tilts her head
the wrong way.

My fingers tingle, itch for the soft
touch of those shoots,
how her naked scalp must feel,
her baby self shown off.
The unkempt roots are exposed,
highlights reaching out
to touch one shoulder, nape
of her neck, the side of her face
that crumples up, waiting to finish
that sentence.

2

'They kept the sirens silent and I pinched
      my left thigh to see if
it was a hearse I was in and later I checked
      the blue smudge to see if
I was still here,' she tells me for the third time.

3

She listens to the language, learns new words
like *oedema* and *meninges*, learns how to find
the noun that counts, the too seductive
painkiller, the one the white-haired nurse says
will hold on to her a breath too long.
She navigates this new city carefully, on wheels,
feels five of her toes push against a light breeze,
not let past the check-in desk, passport control
looking for one solid diagnosis, an explanation,
the reason for her swollen membranes,
her cerebellum peeling back layer through layer,
the hole in her memory taking everything in,
unfillable.

4

The questions I want to ask aren't the ones my mouth pops out—
how's the food?
any hot doctors?
need some more DVD's?

One question charges through my brain,
so hard that my voice goes on autopilot,
seeks out safe ground, floats around the edges of
this question: *how much longer?*

As in how long will she be stuck
on this bed in this room
in this city-state called a hospital
and bigger still, how much longer?

5

'Well as long as you want,' she says.
'I'm not forcing you to stay.' Straight to
pissed off—

from *how much longer* to *what the fuck do I care
I'm only stuck in this damn bed for god knows
how long waiting for everyone to decide*

*when I get to see them, whether I want to or not,
and then there's the five who couldn't bother
their arse coming all the way over to this side*

of the island to see me and me on my holidays,
and we're both laughing and it's okay
because she has already forgotten the question.

6

Goodbye catches in my throat
when I see the time and think of the trip back—
past the smell of St Rita's ward
(a mix of toilet and sticky plasters),
down the lift that didn't get stuck the last time,
out into the safety of the stale city air—
but when my foot moves the only thing
I can come up with is *see you later*
and a quick hug on her feeling side.

Accommodating Grief

The next morning, breakfast.
A slice of buttered toast, just the edge
nibbled off. Scalding tea, as hot as
I can take it.

To the mass I wear a straight black skirt,
just below the knee, calf-length boots
with a low heel. An aubergine cardigan,
to keep me warm.

Three days later I can't call to mind
what I wore the morning he died.
What I ate for breakfast.

Where do I go to find him now?
The graveyard, the chair he sat in
to watch TV, his worn-scented wardrobe?
Or the kettle, the toaster, the routine
space we shared?

Breakfast: a slice of buttered toast,
the crusts trimmed off. Scalding tea,
as hot as he could take it.

On the Fault Line

An east wind blew through the house
that they had fought over for years,
so it sat empty, soulless
for half a decade while homes grew
up around it, springing up out
of half-acre sites like mushrooms.

She lit the range for the first time.
The smoke that billowed out for hours
choked her throat as she scraped away
the soot, caked there for years.
When the dead crow fell down
through the chimney she thought

and this will be home.

Who Knew?

That your house would come
on two trailers,

that your house on two trailers
would come equipped with a yellow toilet,
yellow phone, and gold nylon carpet
that would burn your children's limbs,

that you would know when
the two halves of your house
had the board and tarp pulled off,
they would slot together so
you would never see the join
on the aluminium cladding,

that you would marry him,
move to his home, forget
to get insurance then
burn his house down,

all so your new home could be
delivered on two trailers,
curtains and all.

Coming Home

1

The doctor says it has spread.
My early days bloom every time
I close my eyes, red dots
of cherries we stole from Fox's tree.
The mischief splits and splits,
faithless; shows me the parts
of myself I didn't know
I had, lit up on x-rays
as shadows. Gives me the guts
to spill myself, release
the real me on the world,
spit out the pips.

2

The bed holds me, without
much comfort, cast in solid
iron for my first home.
It weakens every year. Rust spots
stain the joins, show up
through each new coat of paint,
as though we share the same fate,
this half-life a secret we slip
between each night. I sit slowly
for my morning sup of tea,
wish this is the last bed
I sleep in.

Email Me

(for maimeog@iolfree.ie)

The only thing I know about death
is what happens to the body you will leave
behind—stopped pulses, synapses,
connections dropped mid-thread.

But where will you go when your body
stops, when you leave it behind,
to be buried in blue ?

Will you hang out with Granny, give out
to her the lifetime you missed?
Or will you find new people,
the outer reaches of space?

Will you fertilise the souls
still housed in the bodies on earth,
free to nourish the part of us that counts?

Will your soul atoms seek out like,
cluster together, create strength,
almost visible on damp West of Ireland days,
on days when the world seems

dank and useless, and I am swamped
by everything I don't know?

Fireproof

The fire couldn't burn
the faith out of me.
I would stand back, watch
the blaze lick the windowpanes,
picture my Elvis 45s
melt into mounds of vinyl.
I would absorb the scent of charred
television, cushion, pram,
and as the colours developed,
the roaring sound that goes
with red, orange, hot blue electrics.

The next day, I would get up,
prepare breakfast in my in-law's house,
leave piles of coins in the fridge
for each egg I used, mounds of quiet
surrounding each movement.
Noting the wavering colours
of loss and apples, I would step
around another's children,
find a map for each route,
dress my own girls for this new day
in borrowed clothes.

I would teach them
the art of resurrection,
how to rise up out of the flames.
Show them how to bury the ashes,
start a new fire.

Notes

Fired Clay—lines in italic are quoted from the poem 'Boukhara' by Yvonne Green

Totems—Emily Carr (1871-1945) was a Canadian artist (and writer), and is known for her paintings of the totem poles of British Columbia.

The Sleepwalkers—*'Chaque époque rêve la suivante'* translates as 'Every epoch dreams its successor'.

Footfall—Saint Florian is the patron saint of Poland (and fire-fighters). His feast day is May 4.

The Homestead I—'White Field Hill' is a translation of *Sidhe Fionnachaidh*, the fairy mound where the mythical Lir made his home.

Plastic Bags and Cigarettes on the Straits of Moyle—the quote that opens the poem is from Sam Dooher.

Telepathy in Ordinary Lives—Frederic William Henry Myers first coined the term 'telepathy'.

About the Author

Celeste Augé was born in Canada in 1972. She was raised in the backwoods of Northern Ontario until her family moved to Ireland, where she has lived since she was twelve years old. In 2006, she published her first chapbook of poetry, *Tornadoes for the Weathergirl*. Her poetry has also been included in the anthology *The Ground Beneath Her Feet* (Cinnamon Press, 2008) and in the chapbook *Smoke and Skin* (Lapwing). She has been Writer-in-Residence with an after-school programme in Galway, supported by the Arts Council and the National Youth Arts Programme. She has read her work at Cúirt International Festival of Literature, at Galway City & County libraries, at Poetry Ireland's Introductions series of readings, and at other literary events around Ireland. Her poetry was short-listed for a 2008 Hennessy Literary Award. She lives in County Galway.